SOUNDINGS

SANDY CUNNINGHAM

ACKNOWLEDGMENTS

My thanks to Hamish Cunningham, without whom this book would not be appearing online, and with love and gratitude to my wife Eithne for her inspirational and detailed advice.

In memory of Eithne's son, Nathaniel Henson, 1964-2013.

Cover photo, High Force, by Robert Cunningham

Contents

HIGH FORCE: DROWN-FALL..5
NORTHERN BEACH: GHOST COMPANY...6
EASTER: WHOLLY GHOST..8
FAMILY VOICES..10
VOICES BACK WHEN..12
EMBODIED SAYING...13
WATER MUSIC 14
LIKELY, HOODED...15
THRIFT IN FLOWER...16
SUN SETTING...17
HUSHING...18
DUSK BEACH..19
MAKING WORDS MEAN...20
NOCTURNE...22
AUBADE 23
SERENADE..24
DROWSE-THINKING...25
MIND MUSIC...26
DUSK-SELF..27
MIND'S TIDES...28
OUR INWARDLY TALKATIVE BEING..29
AUTUMNAL 30
BEING AND QUIET..31
INSPOKEN...32
TO ALL APPEARANCES..33
SUNSET: TAKING PLACE..34
EVENING...35
THINKING, SAYING, QUIETING..36
EVENING AFTER-THOUGHTS...37
TIDAL...38
REVERIE: WHEREVERNESS...39
SPIDERY..40
OUR VOLUBLE INNER SELFHOOD..41
DROWSE-THINKING...42
EVENING: BECOMING 43
CRUSOE TO CALIBAN,...44
AT JOHN DONNE'S DEATH-BED...47

HIGH FORCE: DROWN-FALL

Gulping, whooshing, out there, as if thrashing
inside our heads, tirelessly vengeful, angrily
drown-craving, plashing, rock-forced, bespeaking
terror, wordless, gulping, clamorous, cold,
as we topple head-to-foot, watching our own
slow, gulping, after-drowns, in some night's
fright, dream-screened, knowing the while
it is not really so, yet compulsively
seeking proof, perversely subject to two lives
        at once, one fictive, one out there, hard, high, forced.

NORTHERN BEACH: GHOST COMPANY

Old friends, long thought-of, drift close by,
below steep east-facing weary cliffs;
ghost beings in the mind's eye, tenebrous.

They hearken to each pebbly clash,
tide-swirl, intricate, anarchic,
which seems to seek what it might mean to say.

Exhilarant, whisper-wording, chattering
speaklets: dissonant, vowelly
swush; gawp drownings; nightmare fright.

Stranded, in compound joy-dread:
horizons misted under; foghorn blares;
failing to trust whichever way we choose.

Finding the rough cliff-path, long-forgotten;
beside oneself with many fancied lost.
Footsteps felt as if by someone else.

Companionable ghostlings, welcome
absentees, as we might seem to them.
Presences astir in mind, that ocean where

promptly, at a touch, they live who ceased to be.
Knowings beset with strangehood;
inhilarating dread; strange joys of menace.

Familiar, odd, each foggiest idea;
dream faces, known, like fadings after sleep.
For good and all, way back, till who knows when?

Good-humoured, wicked, childhood pals;
trashy pranks, on a backstreet spree.
Laughing, rummaging among hot, lusty secrets.

Penumbral, stealthy night-shades;
coal-seamed, grit-syllabled modes of speech;
closing in, distant, inwardly audible.

Living delight in what is yet to know…
we, other-wise, sometimes with only the mistiest
grasp of what on earth or why we live to seek.

Blood-stream think-surfing, brinking, dawn to dusk.
Behaving tidally as wave-words drift at sea.
Daunted; at play; becoming; happening to be.

EASTER: WHOLLY GHOST

'Nothing! thou elder brother ev'n to Shade!'

Shushing, whisht, whooshening
on the quiet, Unbeing of self-substance
with strange Neverywhere, so to whisper-speak!

We chance upon You, from our time to
Your untime, invoked in such vernacular
archaic spokens as might seemly praise you

wherenever You might vague be thought to be.
Luminous, numinous, you bell-wether us,
on each unfenced, gorse-bracken upland

of the mind. Our daunted words bespeak
the ghostly inaudible creaking quietude
of stone walls easing, such rheumatic

whisperings as well might inwardly sound
intimations of You, abstract, else, Nowhere,
cherished Nothing, haloed be thy Name!

Intimations, craves, intimidations:
we, given to naming, beliken You
to anything 'down here' we choose to make You seem.

We, chancy, wordy, ceaselessly begonning,
familiars of Ever, craving any such words
as let us hear what Still seeks how to say.

Shooshing, chanting, draughty, incarnating.
Coded in opaque ritual ologies.
Fought over in sectarian wordy wars.

Inward, outlandish, bleak, You, dreeing our dark weird.
Personified at will by such as we,
and hence, imposing Nowt, unable not to be.

Epigraph from Rochester, 'Upon Nothing'

FAMILY VOICES

'Bucketting down with sleety rain, no call
to be out at large this late, sump wet,
night rising, sea-fret drizzling in
off the crumbling cliffs, nithering cold.'

Relishing swoops of inventive word-play.
Threats masking needy kindness, heart-felt, warm.
Neighbourly backyard helping to make do;
eager for anything to put her hands to.

Insistent present participles, keeping
speaking feeling warm. We, bletherskiting
without having that much needing to be said.
Keen, making shift to quicken a slowing day.

Word-mining, coining, scintilling, instilling;
airy, touching, rhyme-inventing, trilling.
All we half-meant to say, when its time came,
lives on as if hearing itself being said.

Night clouding under, dour, some slow tomorrow.
Back-lane capers, dog yelps, fighting, skelping.
Hard-weathering, dawn, dusk, seagull calls.

We long for elsewheres, cherishing long gones.
Chancing on purposes, randoms of dream,
envying sea-bird whims, eager to drift.
Growing up needful, craving love's carnal feast.
Restive, seeking what might never quite stay found –
One self merging two, joy, sticky-loined, warm.

Soundings; learning to find words for whatever may
cherish the glint-spray of our tidehood lives –

cliff-clinging, dusk-betiding, welcoming ghosts.

See – good-natured, conspiring childhood pals,
laughing at furtive capers, on a backstreet spree,
rummaging, nudging, among dusky secrets.

Blood-streamed think-surfing, brinking, dawn to dusk,
tidally mesmerised, as wave-words break, at sea.
We, moonstruck, biped, happening, always yet to be.

VOICES BACK WHEN

'I've gone and fetched my fist a rare bad narp
on that wonky backdoor sneck that's still to mend.
There's more to do with life than moan and harp.
Try swilling the backyard from end to end.'

'The coal man always chooses our backlane
when my washing, wringing wet, is just hung out.
It'll be the rag-and bone man next, sleet, rain.
What you can't have you can't complain about.

'I've not had time to cross the front-door step
this live-long day, let alone scrub it down.
Siren, black-out, air-raid warden, yet
another night, bombs, rubble, half the town.'

Now, footloose ghosts, me among them, shushing the beach
traipsing about, thinking of wheres and whens, in starts
of old-young dread, spewing, drowning, way out of reach,
toying with sprightly word-play, called 'flashes of clarts'.

'When it comes to the last duff coal, nutty slack,
the short wait in-by for the last cage back -
no two ways about it, all said and done,
.
You're never hard done by till Big Nowt has won.'

That said, let's relish all kinds of being-saying.
 Merriment, fortitude, sprightly abuse of words .
We, biped, present participles, hinting, playing.
With nudges, fudges, inside-out speaks – earthly songbirds.

Seaham Harbour

EMBODIED SAYING

Lend me a hand a bit, we need to
knuckle right down to this awkward job
and make a proper fist of it for good and all.

Hush, listen: ghost voices, forthright, keen,
having their say, inwardly, now as then,
whole-hearted, people from long when agone.

You have nobody but yourselves to blame,
moping about, wet through, as if there's nowt
worth while but yammer and complain.

Never at rest, in fizzing earshot,
keen flicks of speech, thought ligameants,
insisting, as words will, stravaiging about.

If you want a spuggies ticket for the match,
shin up the fence beyond the bowler's end:
it's daylight robbery paying to get in.

Hushed, random, nattering ceaselessly,
synaptic memory-flashes, the body's mind,
soliloquising into silence.

Lilting phrases, dying falls, speech echoes,
busy in wordy mind-shades, talkative,
compulsive: the whispery Now that is Then.

spuggies ticket: the sparrow gets a free view, for which we would
have to cheat our way in.

WATER MUSIC

Seeking apt syllables, runlets, so as to speak
water itself; lucent glimpsings; inflorescence;
seemingly wilful, but in thrall to stream-bed
pebbles, watery wish-falls, wavery weeds.

The looked-at quiet of whatever stirs
unseen, unspoken in our heads, busily
seeks in its turn to have its wordy say,
for all our need for true instillingness.

Stillness we needy crave, not the mere lack
of what to listen to, or seek to say.
Enviably, intimately, breezes frisk-think,
astir in green flicker-leaves, this being their way.

Things we find words for are at once both more
and less identified with what we have them say.

LIKELY, HOODED

Out of all likelihood, the look of a sound
steals in on the quiet, sight unseen;
wrinkled curl-edged thoughts, mouldy-minded,
word-locked, almost about to, seeking
to mean to say, that somewhat different.

Sensory leavings, autumnal smoulders,
faded from eyeshot, somewhere drowsy
inside mind, reflexive, needing to say
how they might truly alter into said.

THRIFT IN FLOWER

Frugal, needy, at its bright wits' ends, aglow,
in salt-scoured seaward cliff-clefts, sea-pink.
Making shift, wincing, snuggled in tufty grassbanks

for sheer thirsty life, parching, sipping scant
bitter runlets, making do; home to peckish
sanderlings, quarrelsome sea-gulls,

that rummage among sharp scraps of tinny
human rustage … short shrift! flowers trying
in dry earth to slake shuddering root-thirst,

precious nothing to drink, hard as that needs be.
Braving all seasons, like my mother greeting want,
well-used to saying, playful, still astir though gone,

'ah well, it's back to porridge and old clothes!'
Shy-proud, averse to being praised, keen
to tease, make-believe; living draughtily

within earshot of the rhythmic, daunting
energies, threats, of wilful cliffs and sea.
Making good, patching, skilfully making do.

SUN SETTING

Preclusive glory desubstantiates
that else-known western hill, hazily backlit
ever-lessenings, endurings, durings.
Time warps, beforewards, on the afterhand.

Above the fictive west, failingly pale,
sky landscapes: cold legendary lakes,
cloud ridges, vaguening hills, dense umbrage.
Gradual elsewheres, time-chilled, merge, emerge.

Elegy, desire, touch-would longing,
perpetual elsewhens, palpable, fictive:
each and every of whom we might have
been, might yet bespeak, figures of new speech.

Seclusion, occlusion, otherwise unsaid.
Over our shoulders, easterly, twilight wisps
of sighing cirrus, wistfully mimicking
the fadings of late fire, dawnings in us, on us.

HUSHING

Duskfall: a wispy sea-fret mystifies
the spell-bound hush of silence, whispering
whatever thought might seek to feel to say.
Remainders, remindering; shaly pit-waste
streaming dry-wavy on the endlong beach.
Long after the last mine-shift has up and gone.

Sea-coal, cold sea; the Featherbed Rock
fallen through, become a lashed sea-stack
by 'preferential erosion', as our
dwarfish geology nerves our dread to say.
Ripple-chuckles; sly dusk; chill draught-thought
'Abackabeyont': mistified finishing touch.

DUSK BEACH

Punctual, moonstruck, all too soon,
below this east-facing weary cliff,
stealthy night-shades, glooming, tenebrous.

Grit-syllabled, clash after pebbly clash,
tide-bound, intricate, foam-seethe seeking
whatever we might take the sea to say.

Sense-defying, wordifying, salty
speechlets, dissonances, vowelly
swirls, speak drownings, nightmare panic.

Stranded in the mind's dread, we seek
horizons misted under (fog-horn blares)
failing to turn whichever way is lost.

Seeking the crumbling cliff-path, beside
oneself with vaguely stranded dead.
Footsteps feeling trod by someone else.

Companionable phantoms, long agone
in their penumbral seeming, near at hand.

MAKING WORDS MEAN

Time, ticking under, steals in on the quiet:
all we might re-dream, by mindsight ... unspoken
colloquies we take inventive tries at,
making words mean more fully, not just betoken.

For all that we can know, or think we might,
each eager light with its own darkness fraught,
inward estrangehood, half-said, shadowy-bright,
seeks to bespeak whatever lurks in thought.

Words constitute what they just seem *about*,
that which recedes, clears, tries to keep in view:
complexing meanings, verges, shadows of doubt,
velleities, misunderstandings, thinking through.

Shush! Our craving how to speak what can't be said,
suggestive lineaments of shady sense,
re-constitutes live speech from thought gone dead:
incursions on that shadowy Immense

which lurks, to perpetrate bright sense, afresh!
Vibring, quick, gallivanting thought,
webbed in its necessary wordy mesh,
spidery-vigilant, seeks what might be sought.

Hearkening to, deciphering its own
inaudible mono-dialogue, the mind,
grounded in dreams which always just have flown;
tentatively past; seeking what future might yet find.

Cherishing every always nearly gone,
although it cannot stay forever found.
Silently activated, mindful, on and on...

inwardly audible, not needing sound.

Readying us to speak without bad faith,
quietude steeps us in attentiveness;
inventively ghosting us, our inward wraith,
courting the flicker-while here-now, eager to guess.

NOCTURNE

Time Beings

Drift-thought, bodily mind-warps, whisperings;
smoulders of touch-would, brushy wisps of thought.

Forebodings, admonishings, belatedly
surfacing, mooding, in the draughty dusk.

Time warps, entrancing, daylight's aftergone.
Moss-glow stream bank, watery swirls of dream.

Intimidations, evening dread-seeps, nearing dark.
Familiar estrangings, alienated whoms.

Selves we have severally, every one of us,
from time to time sought how to be.

Childhood spider-dread from creepy long ago;
fly-paper glue-deaths in the gas-light's whisper.

All we have forgotten not having known 'for real',
rummaging thoughts without a mind to say.

Being, here, now, wherever we appear to stay;
momentous, hungrily seeking what our ghosts might see.

Cherishing frights, adrift in waves of dream.
Unmapped horizons, ventures cast aground.

After-sights, forethoughts, gleams, as if each instant seeks
to loom, luminous, in or beyond all likelihood.

Dusking, selving, musing, *adagio ma non troppo.*

AUBADE

Coming to, From Where Else

Dreams, half well-known as dreamt, while being dreamed.
Heart-felt, their dawning haze-light clears, to be
decoded, thought into: fables our inner Whom
tells, to bespeak itself, the coinage of craved fiction.
Portentous, vividly fading, peculiar:
slow-begone emblems of need, fright, or Nothing itself!

Theatrical, half-palpable, our very own
cherished 'head movies'. Hard to convey
tellingly to our daylight selves quite why
and whithersoever they teem with scraps,
odds, ends, chilling sweats, obsolete shames.

Dreams! accredited anciently as Other-wise.
Dramatis personae, staging their burdensome
opaquely significant scripts! Self-hooded,
leading us elsewhere, towards, astray.
Dawn? let's laugh ourselves back to jovial sleep,
indulging drowsy lovers' wakeful souls,
cosying up in play, snug whisperers:
two-fold, one-minded, other-whoms we!

SERENADE

Language, Loved

Dusking: fewer and fewer greens of inward shade
accord with drowsy notes of soft-sung need,
hushingly gradual, melodic, swathed
in tensely idling calm, the not-yet-said.
Music, enhancing yet assuaging, time-bound,
sooth-singing what it wantonly makes-believe.
The disciplines of rhythm, rhyme, and lies
throb at the very heart of being true.
The culture of pursuing every theme,
requiring that we honour how each ought to sound,
loving the craft that courts our tune-struck dreams.

DROWSE-THINKING

Vague flux of dusklight, chilly inset of dark.
Foreboding after-fulgence, hindsighting.

Whisperish, tenebrous, seemingful, elsewhere.
Keeping a wistful tryst with what stays gone.

Drowsy-scanned half-thoughts, seeking to say
how it would feel *to be* entire blank, *not.*

We *are* whatever shifty dread creeps in upon us,
forebodings of some future inward past,

Dingy after-shadows of foreboding,
seeking what's yet to happen in what's past.

Inwardly keen to speak light's drowsy fades,
the mind crafts multiple metrics out of what?

Tense-bound, in mute or spoken thinking,
despite our eager wishing to speak free.

Darkness in the mind's eye promptly falling,
after-boding, dusking, thoughts inwardly *said.*

MIND MUSIC

Water Falling

Grace notes, *a piacere*, the plink-
plink of *staccato* droplets, crotchetty

suspirando in the rhythmic lift and fall
of cliff-side breeze-whim creepers; dizzy waves

in the mind's own giddy sight as its view
switches from the torrent cascade, out there.

Vivace, bravura dissonances, to
breeze-whim *cantabile*, or to tremulous

tristful *basso profundo* in the head.
Stringy sound-waves, heady chords, lachrymose

dolours, *rallentando* toyings at the edge
of so-called total silence, unattainable, *apaisé*

inside the mind which looks to find peace Other-wise.
Cadent, fall, the sonorous and crotchetty alike.

In quietude, the mind delights
in scanning itself, like owl-cries in thick dusk.

Maestoso, agitato, capriccioso, fast or slow.
Music, in words which sing how it should go.

DUSK-SELF

Whispering, tenebrous, seemingful elsewhere;
fade-set sun; ingoing mindset of the dark.

Hindthought, the after-shadow of foreboding;
blurred outgone of brisk thingwardness of day.

We live, whatever shifty dread creeps in upon us;
shadow-bodings of some future fading past.

Sights gradually duskening, infulgent;
lessening might-beens, dusky still-to-comes.
Inwardly keen to speak light's drowsy fades,
the mind crafts multiple metrics out of where?.

Hereinafterforth, trifling or deepening,
multiple-tensing beings as we inward are.

Findings of selfhood, feel-known, as we seek
to sense each other's lifehood in their very own.
Knowing they know us as we can but guess.
Successive intimations nudging, 'so to speak,yes!'

Thoughts inherently speech-crafted; deep dusk
displacing intrusively what light made of us.

MIND'S TIDES

Tidal aforethought, merging with ebbing
already-said, shore-footed. Sand-blown
ridges, left by gone waves; *maestoso*
under-murmurs, wildering elsewhens.

Sounds warp, thinks rustle, *extempore* grace-notes
chuckle in the mind's hearing, haphazard.
Stage-whispers in a darkling whereafter.
After-bodings, querulous befores.

Familiar, mind's inner self-estranging
looks to think intimately of non-entity.
Time and again, spindrift on mental shores
sizzles; half-saturated tide-marks, the afters of befores.

OUR INWARDLY TALKATIVE BEING

Each of us our own wordy silence, inwardly
curious, where we rake over foresaids, afterthinks,
each of us singularly compound, self-
seeking, word-imperfect, now-and-gone.

Becoming such as we have already
thought to have been, a kind of dream-stirring,
drift-would becoming, whatever
the quick body has its own mind to make us

do, make say, inwardly ghosted by what-on-earth
opaquely lives us in the cloaked, shifting
emptihood of all this gone-coming Time.
No sooner docked than cast-off, ocean-gone.

Adrift, where we rake over foresaid, afterthought,
feelingly distant, palpably intangible;
thinking over, leafing through, each sidelong drift.
Unspeakable mouldy dreads, autumnal, frost.

Within us, night by day, the least speakable
strangeness cries to be heard, craves,
to clarify about us what must still recede.
Finding, saying, thirsting strangely for more need.

Knowing all this reflexively, outside-in,
we eagerly seek becoming what we say.
Befriending syllabic radicals, lucky word-root rhymes.
Playfully irresponsible, for goodness' laughing sake.

AUTUMNAL

Sycamore leaves, clinging post-humously
in gutters, anywhere they fall, sump-wet,
freaks of each desultory swishing breeze, as if
our chilly mind's eyes caused them to,
for stray delight, as our clammy thoughts themselves
flip over.

Haphazard wince-winds, flicking
outside-in, slivers of shivering damp
dread, sluggish in gutters as we think
at random, seeking to imitate
what interplay of swirling and inert
might plausibly feel all too true
for such Time Beings as we live, or seem,
through all felt weathers, seasons, awake like dream.

BEING AND QUIET

The visibly audible flutter within flames;
inward soliloquies, glancing light;
wordily seek-saids, half-catching on;
nerving us to bespeak, alter, gainsay,
what on earth outfaces us, all eyes,
from the cloaked emptihood of all this time.

Aforesight merging into hinter-thought;
chancy syllabics, lucky word-root rhymes;
sidelong meaning-drifts, teetering to be said
out loud, from quietude, dawned on us in dusk.
Meanings-ful moments, night or day, clear or obfusc.
Chancy or managed, random verse or rhyme.

Tell-tales enacted in rhymical mime;
Figures of arcane speech, known as the Self.
Embodied in privately risible ways
which we laughably cherish, cloaking our shames.

INSPOKEN

Meaning to Say

Far to seek, becoming near to find;
unheard-of, suddenly within reach;
inexpressible, nimbly bespeaking itself:
the act of saying finds what who means to say?

TO ALL APPEARANCES

Quick, fleetingly visible, here then gone
as we fancy them, foreshadowed,
but promptly, almost already, after-thought.

Concurrent mental seasons, momentary
years, precede what has already just occurred!
Each of our sensings ghosted by some abstract
cherished idea, on earth as we think of heaven!

Corporeal, engrossing visions, generated by
our quick mortality. Though neither here nor
where, we can at will, at once, live both!
Embodiments of minding our carnality.

SUNSET: TAKING PLACE

'Our' sun, manifestly, so to say and think,
diminishes, beyond our seeming place 'down here',
where we seek to make outmost What explicable,
'dark matter' not excluded, 'cosmic dust'
domestically-titled, in our homely
sweep of thinking, drifting far 'up somethere'.

Light's daily stage appearances, on time,
'heaven-sent' in our mortal, cherished
mythical metaphor. We, spooky astrologers,
superstitious about doom, foretelling darkly;
anxious, facing nothing, in our temporal
hubristic, cloudy, time-bound souls!

We, figures of speech, keenly empirical,
entranced by cosmic metaphors, brave-minded,
littoral, on eternal oceanic shores;
given to asking tirelessly, 'down here',
how 'bubble-blowing black holes' came to rule
galaxies; but living our earthly narratives, while
smiling at fake suffixes: mortalistic, funerable,
chuckle-wordy, jocundated, laughing fit to cry!

EVENING

Selves Inwardly Speak

Promptly here and gone, dusk, theatre of hind-sight:
after-effects of foreboding, shades
newly-seen, frail wisps of knowing;
unvoiced half-memories of long-unsaids.

Foregones themselves rummage among new dreads:
echo-chambers vibrant with not-spokens.
Shadowy truths underlie random fancies,
bethought without being minded to express.

Innermost strangers to our very selves:
hind-thought, antecedent memory, glades
everlastingly deciduous, as if
what we forget outlives its own demise.

Under-during wisps of latent knowing
constitute us more than we know we know.
Mutations of quietude, longing
to come clear from all the talkative rest.

Carnal thought, joys of our own desiring.
We feel for, learn, one another, touchily,
by heart, familiar also with instrangement;
wishing each tense came clear of all the rest.

Times out of mind, as mind itself reminds us,
quick flesh thinks nimbly what it means to say.
Sprightly embodiments, carnal souls,
temporal wizardries by night as bright as day.

THINKING, SAYING, QUIETING

We, inside-loud, thought-by-thought, gone, to come, new-fangling
our selves at the cumulo-nebulous
'if only' edge of pre-monition, wish or need,
wondering how to bespeak fragments of possibles
at large in the Self, that weird, unconstant entity which we
make many of, each one our very own,
whether amorphous or stone-hearted, cloudy or clear,

each being dauntingly other, but
equally self-hooded, human, for good and, or, all.

Insight lights us, wakeful, to feel others-wise,
sensing, if never perfectly, each new
equally-needy selfhood, riddlingly also whom?
Each at home in its protean turnstile wantonness.

EVENING AFTER-THOUGHTS

Westering gones; dusky narratives of hind-thought.
After-effects of foreboding, shades
fleetingly seen during wisps of knowing.

Echo-chambers vibrant with not-spokens,
bethought without our having the mind to think.
Fanciful truancies teeming with home-truths.

Foregones themselves rummage among dark dreads.
We, innermost strangers to our very selves,
countenance them, mirror them, with fresh surprise.

Selfhoods, familiars of our inward eyes,
which need and yearn to be more truly others-wise.
Seeking to read them by their very own inward light,

like darkness, still to penetrate, alluring.
Concluding that we think, inhabit, states of during,
cherishing after-thoughts, relishing mind-sight.

TIDAL

Unspoken

Self-willed ideas, as the body seeks
 to make up its mind, somewhere awash
with runnels of thinking; forgetfulness
remembering having thought so before.

Prevocatively merging thought with aftersaid,
on the quiet. Foreboding, slow betides,
vowelly spindrift, talkative randoms
of streaming water-thinking speech.

Consciousness inherently seeks elsewhere,
eager to find what that says as itself.
Inner tidal dithers, missing the drift;
brain-wash hesitance, garrulous quiet.

Out of sight is into mind, each next thought
awash with how it might possibly be said.
Whirl, rush, or quietude, contemplative;
thought about thinking, unspoken prolific speech.

REVERIE: WHEREVERNESS

Minutely dwelling on so-called timelessness,
vaguening tide-waves, wavering vagues,
darkening brain-swim, randomly, shadening,
knowing full well what we emptily say,
might put thoughts in the right mind to be said.

SPIDERY

Peripheral half-seems, touchy
insistences, attend us portentously,
spider-webby corners of dusty window-frames.

Wispy, whispery hearsaids. deep in whomever we be,
attend us portentously, a ghosted
dream-script making up our minds, bidden or unbidden.

OUR VOLUBLE INNER SELFHOOD

Inwardly heard-seen thought-speech, mind-currents,
whose volatile, draughty, talkative silence
characterises each of us, time after time,
insistent, spell-binding, true.
Deep selves resist, elude, our ardent
craving, in good faith, to be wholly known.
Not that our inward, many-selved monologues
impede our felt each-ness, by craft or chance.
Recondite mind-candour, truthful and make-shift,
both at once! Needing to know wholly
what we cannot wholly know! Seeking, adrift!

DROWSE-THINKING

Vague flux of dusklight, chilly inset of dark.
Foreboding after-fulgence, hindsighting.

Whisperish, tenebrous, seemingly elsewhere.
Keeping a wistful tryst with what stays gone.

Drowsy-scanned half-thoughts, seeking to say
how it would feel *to be* entire blank, *not.*

Foresight, thought's fanciful projector.
Intentions overgrown with might-not-be.

Dingy after-shadows of foreboding,
seeking what's yet to happen in what's past.

Tense-bound, in mute or spoken thinking,
despite our eager wishing to speak free.

Inwardly keen to speak light's drowsy fades,
the mind crafts drowsy metrics out of what?

Darkness in the mind's eye promptly falling,
after-boding, dusking, thoughts inwardly *said.*

EVENING: BECOMING

Dusk, more than still, or stilled, sun-sinking slow;
Our selves involuntarily becoming stillness.
Self as a someone intimately other,
not just indulging in dusk-drowsy thought,
but being whom one might, dark, inly be.
In-stilling, feeling in tune with the lift and fall
of crinkly, dry-leafed branchlets.
Autumnal-minded, insensibly, numinously,
we, blurring slowly, hushing, hearing our own breath.
Trancing, self-hooded night, its very own
quiet here-elsewhere. We, present, bemused,
wishing to let words free to whisper their own
meanings, while prizing, quietly,
thinking *without* words. We, shadowly,
so to speak, involuntarily take place,
Others-wise, each seemingly oneself. Shades,
spooky familiars, bewitching our own selves?

CRUSOE TO CALIBAN,

proposing racial segregation

That claim you made, "this island's mine!":
let us discriminate
between a man like Prospero
who'll endlessly inflate

with fancy metaphysics his
dark urge to tyrannise,
and humane traders like one's self:
I think you'll realise

that when I talk of Providence
one has in friendly mind
our mutual welfare, in a sense,
as you shall joy to find.

That God loves men both pink and brown
is only half my plea,
for there's another aspect of
responsibility:

a deference, I say, is due
not just to me from you
(as I look up to Providence
for smiling on us two),

but also, by fair inference.
to you from God and me.
You *are* the savage (noble soul),
your standards are not mine,

but caves become unsavoury
when they've been used some time.
I'll send in my removal men,
at my expense, of course,

and my man Sunday who will never
knowingly use force.
It may mean walking in for work,
but hard lines can fulfil

the soul which strenuously trusts
in its Creator's will.
You'll make a new man of you yet,
without my playing stern:

old customs which grow native are
the hardest to unlearn!
Then let us wisely both defer
to differences due

to accidents by which He blessed
some creatures more than you.
I brave the fires of high finance,
you carry in the sticks;

while *you* run after wench and such,
I'll bear the politics:
for never have I been the chap
to prick against the kicks!

I'll build you quarters in the scrub
to shield us from disease,
and welfare zones where you and yours
may take your cruder ease.

So may you (with exceptions) go
the same way as your mother,
while I sit here with Prospero,
my fanciful twin brother.

If every such internal matter
Could be so kindly solved,
the world would see why power upon
the powerful devolved.

AT JOHN DONNE'S DEATH-BED

No busy-body sun peeps in
Upon this strait and narrow bed
Where you lie tidy in your welcome shroud,
A brace of pigeons at your feet
(why should physicians cure what kindly kills?)
to draw off the rheumatic cloud
that aches behind the eyes it cannot blind.
But thunder claps his hands, and loud
through the damp dusk one death-bell mourns mankind.

Theme for a sermon in that bell –
the cramped hand fumbles on an inky page –
as once, after a night of love, the sun
struck you like tinder into rage
against what no pen cures, the fatal sense
that after all is said and done –
the blood's entire delight, time caged in words –
each blinding consummation gone,
delight itself unlocks time's homing birds.

Remembered estacy might once
have bled you – bitter surgery – dry,
but now, immune from flesh and blood's disease,
you crave the final remedy,
the willing spirit seeping through the skull.
Jack's soul has overstayed his lease
in the damp tenement, dismayed to find
filth habitable – now, no peace
until your shut lids make the windows blind.

Stairs creak; tenant leaves aching house
tidy; at thunder-clap of doom
the death-bell shouts for joy; with flailing wings

dead pigeons fly unerring home,
over threshed London. One death reaps mankind.
But if upon this threshing-floor still swings
Equivocal the sun to lovers' eyes,
what shall we do, Dean Jack, when time's wound stings,
who lack Paul's pulpit-fire to cauterize?

Durham 1956 – Wensley 2014

Printed in Great Britain
by Amazon

27604437R00030